PRAISE FOR JACQUELINE PIRTLE

"Jacqueline takes you always directly to what you are ready to see or experience."

— LONGTIME CLIENT AND READER

"It is liberating to face your own blocks and to be finally free of the weight that they have caused for many years. And while for me the changes I'm experiencing are noticeable and real, I still feel like myself. Just a more sure self."

— LONGTIME CLIENT AND READER

"Jacqueline makes me BELIEVE I can be and live a joyful and magical existence every new day of my life!"

— LONGTIME CLIENT AND READER

JACQUELINE PIRTLE
High for Life

The best case scenario!

A 30 day journal

COPYRIGHT

Copyright © 2021 Jacqueline Pirtle
www.FreakyHealer.com

All rights reserved. No part of this book may be reproduced or transmitted in any form or by any means, electronic or mechanical, including photocopying, recording, or by any information storage and retrieval system without the written permission of the publisher, except where permitted by law.

ISBN-13: 978-1-955059-15-2

Publisher: Freaky Healer

Editor-in-chief: Zoe Pirtle
All-round Support: Mitch Pirtle

Book cover design by Kingwood Creations kingwoodcreations.com

Author photo courtesy of Lionel Madiou madious.com

I want to let you know that all my books and holistic practitioner work together are a wholesome system, supporting you to live a more conscious, mindful, and happier life.

However, I made it so you can receive the benefit of living more joyously solely by working through this terrific journal book, while also experiencing the full satisfaction in continuing on to the next journal of this series—not to mention the rock solid tools you get by reading any of my other books or adding in my podcast *The Daily Freak*. Either way, I know you'll love my inspirational teachings.

Find out more at:
www.freakyhealer.com
Amazon Author Page
The Daily Freak Podcast

Before you dive in, I want to thank you for hopping on the magic train with me! I truly hope you enjoy *High for Life* as much as I loved writing it, and if you do, it would be wonderful if you could take a short minute and leave a review on Amazon.com and Goodreads.com as soon as you can.

Your kind feedback helps other readers find my books more easily, and be happy faster. Consider it a happy deed for the world.

Thank you!

ACKNOWLEDGMENTS

Let's be honest here… I have a dream team!

I could not have finished this book without the help of talented, creative, high-for-life, and phenomenal professionals.

From the bottom of my heart, I want to thank Zoe Pirtle for her editorial mastery; Mitch Pirtle for his all-round support; kingwoodcreations.com for their fun and polished book cover design; and madiouART.com for an amazing photo shoot.

I'd also like to extend a huge "Thank You!" to all fans of my work and books—I created this beautiful journal series for you.

Life is spectacular with you on my side!

What's your happy place?
Go there, stay there, and never leave!

DEDICATION

*I dedicate this journal to all those that think that being **high-for-life** is not in the cards, and challenge them to make it **BE** their path!*

INTRODUCTION

Phenomenal *high-for-lifer*,

How cool is it that our paths are crossing—and even better, that together we will create well-feeling, love, happiness, and bliss while thriving to live a life that's worth loving?

High for Life is something I incorporate and talk about in all areas of my work—now, I have even created a journal about it, so let me explain.

High-for-life is a state of being where you are aligned with your true you, your well-feeling, and your happiness—whatever that might be and no matter the circumstances, because sometimes being angry or sad is exactly that. Nothing can inspire you to be anyone or anything else than yourself when you are in your high-for-life frequency. It is a state of constant change that is aligned with the flow of life; and a deeply, securely, rooted-as-yourself way of being and living.

Everything is energy - you, me, this journal, and all of life - and it's all *ONE* and the same: Energy! It's also all connected and shared at all times—meaning that you, living through these high-for-life ways that you are creating in this journal, will spread to everything and everyone lifting the whole world into a higher state, or at least as high as they want to go with you.

As these energies, everything and everyone vibrates in different frequencies—some are higher, like being in wonder about life, while others are lower, like not loving your life. Every scenario always has a high-for-life version as well as a low-for-life version—or one lower than the highest possibility. Embracing all of them is incredibly powerful; however, things get super exciting when you consciously choose which way you want life to be and how you want to feel.

High for Life helps you to see all of the different scenarios that are possible, while dreaming up and feeling your own personal high-for-life preferences for everything at anytime—pushing you to go for the best of the best at all times. There, an ocean of opportunities will catch hold of you, inviting you to latch on. Just think of that incredible match-up and shift into the higher frequency of bliss, by being *ONE* with the excitement of these manifestations.

A high-for-life way of living gives your best version of you the stage and momentum—all while changing at a constant and vivid speed and in the flow with how life naturally happens.

Journaling through this 30 day of *High for Life* brings huge uplifts into the equation so you can experience life like you never have before, craft a time beyond your expectations, and love what you live—to the extent of becoming a master in living consciously and mindfully, feeling phenomenal while manifesting the best of the best. It's a change that is forever!

As a side note, there are a couple of bonus days at the end in case you ever find the need to do two in a day, or so you can keep working while you wait for the next journal in this series to arrive. I also left you a few blank **high-for-life** pages to journal about deepening your ways of being alive.

Enough chit-chat, I know you are ready—so grab your pen

and have incredible fun with catching more life than you have ever caught, in your new crazy ways.

Happiest,
    Jacqueline

 Day 1

IMAGINE yourself standing at the top of a cliff! Don't worry nothing horrible is going to happen, just a little craziness for starters. So on that cliff: you feel powerful and are with clear focus, a still mind, and a neutral heart—you ARE! With excitement you peek up to see the beautiful sky and squint down to see Mother Earth while breathing into these beautiful sights. You are given two choices that are representing two different ways of living. One is to be able to fly freely, lift up weightlessly, and go wherever whenever you want to. It's a chance at being in charge, claiming your birth right to choose, and flying higher than you have ever flown—a scenario of having freedom while fully standing in your power. The other option is to fall freely and land safely wherever the wind blows you—offering freedom but giving up your birthright to choose and fly high. Both possibilities are an essence of being free but number one is a high-for-life experience, whereas the other is of limited value. Please tell me you want to fly! Then, without taking off yet, bathe in your exciting choice and journal about how this feels all while holding your horses until you take off tomorrow.

_____
_____
_____
_____
_____
_____
_____
_____

High for Life - The best case scenario!

# Day 2

TODAY'S THE DAY! Are you ready to fly? Go on, jump! Trust that you can fly, and rise freely into the height of a life that's perfect for you. Claim your birthright to choose for yourself and step into your power of being you. How does that best case scenario feel? What do you see and hear all the way up here? What inspirations are coming in for you? Is your heart exploding with joy, bliss, and aliveness? Are you ready to scream from the top of your lungs, "I AM alive, I AM living, I AM high-for-life"? Waste not a single minute, write about the flight to your best case scenario!

High for Life - The best case scenario!

# Day 3

YESTERDAY WE COVERED YOUR BIRTHRIGHT. Today, we talk about your birth-suit! Why? Because high-for-life resembles your birth-suit perfectly, since you came here to align with who you really are—which at the core is to BE and live highly. So when you feel happy, know that it's your perfect style. When you are laughing, you are in your fitting garment. When you are shedding a good-feeling tear, you're wearing your gorgeous outfit of emotions. When you feel good - no matter the *what* and *why* - you are dressed top notch as YOU because, after all, you are a professional high-for-lifer and it suits you! What's the visual? Write, journaler, write!

High for Life - The best case scenario!

 ay 4

THE WORD *high* comes with an energetic value of high, higher, and highest, and is in direct alignment with your inner you because your soul being is always guiding you to BE your highest self. *High* also includes an essence of better, more, elevated, uplifted, lighter, and purer.

Saying and thinking the word *high*, and feeling its energy, shifts you directly into a high-for-life frequency.

If you hear the word *high* it's natural to look upward, not down, meaning that through the action of looking up you immediately shift to BE upward—and into a higher frequency than before.

How will you consciously align with all the high-ness in life, and at the same time your highest you?

___
___
___
___
___
___
___
___
___
___
___
___
___

High for Life - The best case scenario!

 Day 5

THE WORD *for* is of utmost value when said, thought of, or felt, because it is saturated with positivity—freeing you from resistance, pressure, or any such exhausting patterns. Just think about it; even as an action it ultimately has winning energy attached—you push *for* something. You fight *for* one thing, you go *for* what's aligned with who you really are. *For* is powerful and magical all at the same time! How will you incorporate much more of that *for* you?

High for Life - The best case scenario!

 ay 6

THE WORD *LIFE* is deeply meaningful in your physical department because it speaks of your truth that you are alive—all while letting you expand and calibrate energetically.

Sensing yourself into the essence of *life* means you shift into a frequency of possibilities, love, and excitement, while also into pain, sadness, and anger—because those too belong to being and living a beautiful life.

The act of living is one of change, action, and enjoyment—a beautiful and thrilling shift for you to latch onto and relish in without ever stopping.

How will you be more conscious of *life*—in words, in life itself, and in living your life? Is fully and vividly an option?

___
___
___
___
___
___
___
___
___
___
___
___
___
___
___

High for Life - The best case scenario!

 Day 7

THERE IS NO *ONE-SIZE-FITS-ALL*, ever! High-for-life is very individually felt because everyone is unique and here for their own special reason. Feeling highly also changes every split second, since life is ever-changing and so are you. For some right now feeling high-for-life is happiness, while for others, it is being deeply embedded in sadness; for some it's traveling around the world, and for others it's owning a house. But one thing is always the same and a given—high-for-life means that someone is feeling amazing, satisfied, or over the moon in their life. What is your own special dream right now, today, tomorrow, next week, or in the long run?

_____

High for Life - The best case scenario!

ay 8

HIGH-FOR-LIFE IS a constant and vivid process that's needing your attention on all different levels of your whole being—physical and energetic. How will you make sure to feel physically wonderful? Is better and cleaner food an option, or perhaps a new way of moving? And energetically, how will you listen to your inner you and follow its wisdom—without rolling your eyes at the *sometimes* strange input?

High for Life - The best case scenario!

 Day 9

EVERYTHING IN LIFE has a high end and a low end - plus of course all the different heights in between - giving you endless choices in how you want to experience something or someone. High-for-life means that you align with the best case scenario! What in your world right now do you not love as is? List some of these offenders—realize that the way you perceive them is of a lower value. What would a higher - or the highest - frequency of these happenings look like? How do you feel in those higher ways? Remember; you can fly, you can rise, it's your birthright to choose, and you have the power to BE you.

_____
_____
_____
_____
_____
_____
_____
_____
_____
_____
_____
_____
_____
_____
_____
_____
_____

High for Life - The best case scenario!

 ay 10

A HIGH-FOR-LIFE WAY of living involves your action of actively doing something—like taking off on a spaceship to see limitlessness, parachute jumping to feel the buzz, taking a cold shower to be tough, or being silly to feel like a child again. But it can also be achieved by your powerful ability to imagine, visualize, or feel yourself into a great state. For example; if you are sitting in a boring meeting, start imagining yourself at the beach while feeling the sand between your toes. Voila, your high-for-life is created! What fabulousness do you have up your sleeve—to go from blah to *vive la vie*?

___

High for Life - The best case scenario!

 ay 11

For balance sake, *always* doing something, being active, moving, being out and about, or experiencing out-of-this world cool stuff does not guarantee that you are always feeling high-for-life. Many times it is actually achieved by aligning with yourself in stillness or meditation while doing nothing, being bored, or spending time alone in nature. How can you pay more attention to what feeling good really means? How will you align with yourself more often?

___

High for Life - The best case scenario!

 ay 12

IMAGINE you are hugging the sun while gushing gratitude and love towards it—as a thank you for all the high-for-life'ness it does for you. What would you say to the sun? How would you honor this bright light—is it by beaming yours strongly too, in order to support the sun to make the world even shinier? What else in your surroundings represents such high-for-life thankfulness? Is it a cookie—a smile, a rainbow, some $100 bills, or the sky? What will you say to those things, and how will you celebrate them? Keep choosing new items, people, and happenings—feel how you shift higher and higher while at it!

___

High for Life - The best case scenario!

ay 13

WHAT ON OR inside your physical body represents high-for-life for you? Is it your heart and powerful love, a strain of hair that's playing with your face, your smile giving and catching happiness, a single cell that's keeping you alive, or your muscles that are tough as nails? Pick many, and list how your special parts make you feel while consciously sensing your shift into wellness. Then, think about what you could say to them—for instance, your heart. Would spilling some loving words or a love letter do? Be generous here. After all, we are talking about your glorious physicality!

High for Life - The best case scenario!

# Day 14

YESTERDAY WAS all about the physical, today the energetic! What is the high-for-life value of your inner being—your soul, inner instinct, higher self, however you would like to call it? Is the deep wisdom, the always correct guidance, the constant knowing, or the unconditional and unlimited love that your energetic you has for you? Make your "I love my inner essence" list, and celebrate it to the moon and back—everyday!

*** High for Life - The best case scenario!***

 ay 15

THINK about the tasks in your everyday life, the ones that don't feel high-for-life. Make your "I don't like this!" list—it should be rebellious and fun. Now look at the other end of every task and find the high-for-life version—the *it's fine to do this*, and the *it's still a gift and a chance*. For instance, take cleaning the toilet; nobody really likes doing that, yet, at the other end of "nobody likes this" is the wonderful part of ending up with a clean bowl—and in case outsourcing feels highest, then that's the higher end of this task. There is a high-for-life version to everything and you can choose to find and focus on it—then sense yourself into the higher wellness of it.

_____
_____
_____
_____
_____
_____
_____
_____
_____
_____
_____
_____
_____
_____
_____
_____

High for Life - The best case scenario!

# Day 16

UNDERSTANDING AND ALSO ACCEPTING, respecting, appreciating, thanking, and loving the incredible fact that *everything* belongs to life is a high-for-life way of existing. The good, the bad, and the ugly, as we so beautifully say—it's all present and inclusive. Question is, how do you want to feel? What life do you want to live, and where will you put your focus—since all these controversies exist at all times?

High for Life - The best case scenario!

 ay 17

You get to know yourself inside and out by feeling fully, and experiencing the vivid variety of your emotions—plus, embracing them as part of you belongs to a high-for-life way of living. Feeling freely means that you get really good at feeling yourself into alignment, and brings incredible wisdom about and for yourself, by giving you clues to when you are in the realm of flying high in your power—meaning, you can actually do something about it. Make your emotional list of *feeling good is flying high* and *not feeling good is flying low*, then come up with fitting solutions.

High for Life - The best case scenario!

ay 18

HIGH-FOR-LIFE DOES NOT ALWAYS mean happy. Any lower-frequency feeling starts out as feeling good at first—making it high-for-life at the beginning. Take anger, for example; in the first split second when you are angry it can feel good or at least better than not being angry—then after the initial up, you'll feel down, which is a clear sign that it's time for you to shift to a better feeling. Being angry is not a bad thing and neither is feeling crappy in your anger—however, staying unhappy could be. What feelings don't fit anymore, and what different ones do you desire—ready to shift?

___

High for Life - The best case scenario!

 ay 19

DREAMING up your perfect life is a high-for-life practice with enormous potency attached. It's a way to focus yourself energetically and then have it show up on your doorstep of physicality—that's the case for day dreaming, night dreaming, and all in-between dreams. So visualize, imagine, feel, and write your perfect story! This asks for you to not hold back, but to reach for the stars and way beyond for your wishes and desires. Go on dreamer, make it magical!

High for Life - The best case scenario!

 ay 20

HIGH-FOR-LIFE MEANS that you step into a pair of shoes even if they feel too big to fill—knowing that they only seem big because of your perception of being too little, not deserving, not capable, or being limited. Not because of the shoe being too big. What life puts in front of you and is inviting you to step into is *never* too big for you, instead, it always fits perfectly. "So tell me all about how you feel in these fitting shoes—and living your gigantic life!" says your journal.

_____

High for Life - The best case scenario!

 ay 21

LIVING your life like it's a store in which you are invited to look around, shop for what you want, or order what interests you - while tasting a little here and there, and returning what's not right anymore - is a high-for-life way of existing. The best part is, it's the truth! What is your favorite shop—a clothing place, grocery store, travel agency, or farmers market? How do you behave when you are there, are you excited, feel eager, inspired, expecting, and abundant? Pretend that this store is your life and copy/paste your high-for-life ways into how you live your life.

High for Life - The best case scenario!

 ay 22

PAYING bills can seem like a downer activity: yet even that task has a high-for-life scenario by being an exchange, and every trade means there is a give and take—a balancing essence. But there is more! Paying bills makes the person on the receiving end happy —just like you felt when the goods were received. How will you change your attitude when paying your bills? How can you hold onto those uplifting thoughts, and pay through the energy of high-for-life?

High for Life - The best case scenario!

 ay 23

ALLOWING yourself to be new and fresh at every split second means you are high-for-life—besides going with the natural flow of how life rolls. How will you take this to heart? Is it by letting go of your jeans once you don't like them anymore, by finding different foods to taste deliciousness again, or by figuring out how to get in sync with yourself in a fresh new way? Same with your job, family, or loved ones—how can you be your always new you?

_____
_____
_____
_____
_____
_____
_____
_____
_____
_____
_____
_____
_____
_____
_____
_____
_____
_____

High for Life - The best case scenario!

Day 24

TAKING life by the horns and riding *with* it all wildly and vividly is a high-for-life lifestyle! When was the last time you did that? What will it take for you to go jump into a freezing pool, write the book you always wanted to write, sing from the top of your lungs while not minding who's listening, love whoever you want to love, and feel like the luckiest person alive? Call me crazy—but only until you made your list, because after all, you are one of them too.

High for Life - The best case scenario!

 ay 25

FINDING the high-for-life in your pain is within reach! On the other end of pain there is always a golden opportunity to feel amazing - even when it's acute - by embracing your pain and accepting, respecting, appreciating, thanking, and loving this wonderful signal as the language of your body here to tell you more about yourself. Doing so shifts you into a resistance-free space where healing can take place. Where in your body are you hurting right now? What is your pain telling you, guiding you to do?

___

High for Life - The best case scenario!

 ay 26

FOOD WANTS you to play with it - not fight - because having fun with food is part of being and living high-for-life! You are deeply invited to form a loving relationship with all that goes into your body—water included. So sense yourself into the energy of your food - energizing, clean, nourishing - and notice your automatic shift to the same frequency—making you energetically prepared to digest your food. Tap into how your food will make you feel once you've eaten it, and chit-chat with your food to form an open time of communication. Make your list of high-for-life foods that fill you with energy and aliveness, then keep coming back to add more favorites.

___

High for Life - The best case scenario!

 ay 27

High-for-life means that you find the most powerful and well-feeling way to deal with what's there for you right now while aligning with your strong you—your winner you. Sometimes that means asking for help and allowing that to be your strength—because taking care of your needs IS being strong. Other times, you find strength in doing it yourself even when it is hard—tapping into the power of "dealing with it." Make your list of happenings and strong-like-bull ways—then use the resulting clarity!

High for Life - The best case scenario!

 ay 28

It's good to be your own brave-heart and show up bolder than you were yesterday, or just a minute ago, because you constantly are expanding and calibrating into a higher, wider, and more powerful you. News flash—there is nothing wrong with you, your life, or with others if your *as-it-is* doesn't fit anymore. On the contrary; everything is right with everything, because you have outgrown the old. Bravo! What's getting on your nerves, feels too tight, or is not exciting anymore, and how would a better fitting scenario look like?

___

High for Life - The best case scenario!

 Day 29

FINDING your high-for-life in your lows is possible, because on the other end of all unwell-feeling emotions, there is always the gracious opportunity to feel wonderful even when in the abyss. Accepting, respecting, appreciating, thanking, loving all of you, and allowing how you feel to become your deepest truth barometer creates a space where whole-being wellness has a chance, because there, you get to know yourself really well. Where, with, what, whom, and how are you emotionally stretched? What is your mental state telling you? How can you love all of you?

_____
_____
_____
_____
_____
_____
_____
_____
_____
_____
_____
_____
_____
_____
_____
_____
_____

High for Life - The best case scenario!

 ay 30

HURRAY! You are at the 30 day high-for-life mark! Are you skipping down your path of life? Did you color your hair orange yet, dressing like your own unique crazy you, wearing mismatched socks, or cooking breakfast for dinner and eating dessert as your entree? I hope to hear a "Yes, of course!" Otherwise, it's time to start skipping! What are your best case scenarios for living your crazy cool life?

___

High for Life - The best case scenario!

* * *

Ready to continue on your self-growth path? Get the next journal in this series: ***Bragging: Because you're worth it!***

BONUS

Because hey, nobody ever wants the goodness to end.

Keep on high-for-life-ing because there is never a ceiling!

# Day 31

PICK ONE HIGH-FOR-LIFE THOUGHT, emotion, feeling, activity, act, word, color, treat, scent, view, taste, and happening—small or big does not matter here. List one, or even better, many, then breathe into these high-for-life scenarios, and focus on them for the next 7 days by making them your well-feeling tools—of course, while continuing with a page a day in this journal. After the week is through, come back, and realize how great you feel, and start your next weekly plan while journaling page by page.

___

High for Life - The best case scenario!

 ay 32

CHOOSE one concrete high-for-life essence in nature that shifts you immediately into your higher-than-high place. What is it—an animal, a flower or plant, fruits or vegetables, the sky, the sun, the moon, or the stars, the ocean? Pick a few if that's your jam! How do they make you feel? How will you use these nature-tools as great shifters? Would a T-Shirt with pineapples do—if pineapples are the ones? Or some beach printed socks?

_____
_____
_____
_____
_____
_____
_____
_____
_____
_____
_____
_____
_____
_____
_____
_____
_____
_____
_____
_____

High for Life - The best case scenario!

 ay 33

High-for-life means knowing that you always have unlimited time to stop and smile, laugh, be happy, enjoy, or do nothing else other than being blissful. It takes time to be joyous, just like it takes time to cook, clean, shop, or do your work—so give yourself that time! How will you schedule *happiness* on your day-to-day calendar?

___

High for Life - The best case scenario!

Day 34

NAY-SAYERS, negative-ers, and down-ers! In truth, they are still in their high-for-life frequency - even if it does not look like that from your point of view - because their low could be even lower, making how they are behaving their high-for-life way of being for right now. You are expanding on your own terms and through journaling here you have calibrated into an even higher self—making them seem even lower to you. Great news is that you never have to match where anybody is. Instead, you can keep climbing higher and higher at your own pace while perceiving them being at their highest point possible—shifting them into a higher value for you while sharing that higher energy with them. This way, everyone wins!

High for Life - The best case scenario!

 ay 35

WHAT CHOICES from your past would you not renew anymore, yet still are living? List them without judgment because not only is judging a lower value, but the past is also the past, and you chose what felt best for you back then. There is no need to dig deep into your old decisions or the *what* and *why*. Instead, and with pride say, "I choose new, again, to give myself the best NOW!" Choosing as your power of freedom while flying high-for-life, what newness will you decide for yourself?

_____
_____
_____
_____
_____
_____
_____
_____
_____
_____
_____
_____
_____
_____
_____
_____
_____

High for Life - The best case scenario!

AND NOW IT'S YOUR TURN!

The following are your magical pages to keep cracking your illusionary ceiling of limits!

I'm counting on you to go high-for-life here!

HIGH-FOR-LIFE MEANS...

High for Life - The best case scenario!

Day 37

HIGH-FOR-LIFE MEANS…

High for Life - The best case scenario!

Day 38

HIGH-FOR-LIFE MEANS...

High for Life - The best case scenario!

High-for-life means…

High for Life - The best case scenario!

 ay 40

High-for-life means...

___

High for Life - The best case scenario!

* * *

Don't forget to leave a review on Amazon.com and Goodreads.com as soon as you can, as your kind feedback helps other readers find my books easier. Thank you!

ALSO BY JACQUELINE PIRTLE

365 Days of Happiness

Because happiness is a piece of cake!

This passage book invites you to create a daily habit to live your every day joy, and is the parent companion to *365 Days of Happiness*, the journal workbook.

* * *

365 Days of Happiness - Special Edition

Because happiness is a piece of cake

This beautiful Special Edition of the bestseller ***365 Days of Happiness: Because happiness is a piece of cake*** has room for your notes after every daily passage.

* * *

365 Days of Happiness - Journal Workbook

Because happiness is a piece of cake

This enlightening journal workbook is your daily tool to create a habit of living your every day bliss, and is the companion to ***365 Days of Happiness: Because happiness is a piece of cake***.

* * *

Life IS Beautiful - Here's to New Beginnings

If you like digging deeper into the meaning of life and are inspired by spirituality, then you'll love Jacqueline's effective teachings.

* * *

Parenting Through the Eyes of Lollipops

A Guide to Conscious Parenting

If you like harmony at home and laughter in the house, then you'll love Jacqueline's inspirational methods.

* * *

What it Means to BE a Woman

And Yes! Women do Poop!

If you like to live free, empowered, and want to decide for yourself, then you'll love Jacqueline's liberating ways.

* * *

What. If. - Turning your what IFs into it IS!

A 30 Day or 90 Day - Extended Edition - Journal

If you like to be in charge of your own life, turn your dreams into reality, and enjoy journaling then you'll love Jacqueline's uplifting teachings.

* * *

Open - Where it all starts!

A 30 Day or 90 Day - Extended Edition - Journal

If you like to be open to live your life fully, allow your dreams to come true, and enjoy journaling then you'll love Jacqueline's uplifting teachings.

* * *

To BE and Live - The reason you are here!

A 30 Day or 90 Day - Extended Edition - Journal

If you like to feel alive, wish for your dreams to come true, and enjoy journaling, then you'll love Jacqueline's levitating teachings.

ABOUT THE AUTHOR

Bestselling author, podcaster, and holistic practitioner, Jacqueline Pirtle, has twenty-four years of experience helping thousands of clients discover their own happiness. Jacqueline is the owner of *FreakyHealer* and has shared her solid teachings through her podcast **The Daily Freak**, sessions, workshops, presentations, and books with clients all over the world. She holds international degrees in holistic health and natural living. Her effective healing work has been featured in print and online magazines, podcasts, radio shows, on TV, and in the documentary *The Overly Emotional Child by Learning Success*, available on Amazon Prime.

For any questions you might have, to sign up for Jacqueline's newsletter, and for more information on whatever else she is up to, visit www.freakyhealer.com and her social media accounts @freakyhealer.

www.ingramcontent.com/pod-product-compliance
Lightning Source LLC
Chambersburg PA
CBHW071423070526
44578CB00003B/671